MW00856488

FAVORITE
CASTLES

Ireland

and

Northern Ireland

From
Bargain Travel Europe

Photography and Text
By
Michael January

2014
22.2.22

Winged Lion Publications

ISBN-13: 978-0615832531
ISBN-10: 0615832539

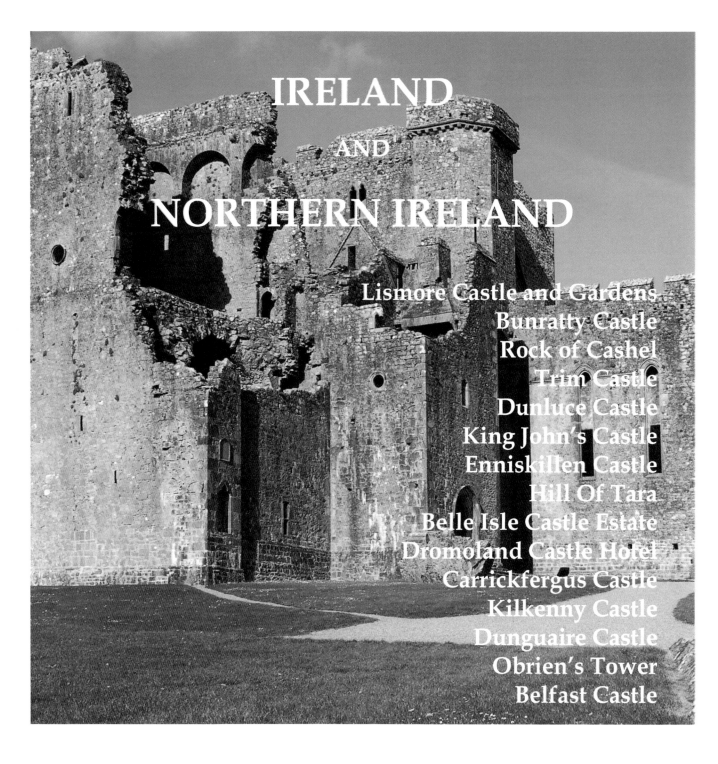

IRELAND

AND

NORTHERN IRELAND

Lismore Castle and Gardens
Bunratty Castle
Rock of Cashel
Trim Castle
Dunluce Castle
King John's Castle
Enniskillen Castle
Hill Of Tara
Belle Isle Castle Estate
Dromoland Castle Hotel
Carrickfergus Castle
Kilkenny Castle
Dunguaire Castle
Obrien's Tower
Belfast Castle

PREFACE

Ireland's castles tell a story of conflict, conquest and the shaping of a society over a thousand years. Most of the medieval castles which remain today in Ireland are the result of the Normans during the reign of the Plantagenet King Henry II and the conquest of Ireland beginning in 1169 lead by Richard de Clare, the 2nd Earl of Pembroke, known as "Strongbow". The Norse Vikings had controlled large part of the coastal areas from Dublin to Wexford and inland to Limerick, in conflict with the Gaelic Irish clan kings. The 12th and 13th centuries were the age of medieval fortress building, with many of the stone structures taking shape under the reigns of King John and Henry III. The next period of building was during the Tudor age of Queen Elizabeth and the revolt of the Gaelic Chieftans, mostly in the north region of Ulster in 1603. This lead to the "Flight of the Earls" and the Plantation of Ireland, when protestants from Scotland and Northern England were seeded lands in the north, resulting in religious conflict and finally the formation of the Republic in 1921, dividing Ireland and Northern Ireland.

The age of gunpowder forced a change in the purpose of the castle, with modifications for cannons, which ultimately ended the days of the great stone forts, which came to ruin during the Parliamentarian period following the English Civil War and the brutal conquest of Ireland under Oliver Cromwell. The Victorian Era brought about the revival of the old castles, reborn as luxurious manor houses. Some castles are government council run national monuments, some are still in private family hands, and some have been reinvented as luxury hotels, but all tell a fascinating story, set in the beautiful and dramatic landscapes of the Irish Isle.

Michael January

LISMORE CASTLE
& GARDENS

Flowering Gardens of Lismore in County Waterford

Lismore Castle in County Waterford is one of southeast Ireland's most lovely castles for its setting, drama and most notably for its gardens. There has been a castle at Lismore since 1185, when a fortress was first built under England's Prince John. When he gained the crown he handed the early medieval castle over to the Bishops of Waterford who used it as a palace up until the reign of Henry VIII. In 1589, the castle was bought by Sir Walter Raleigh, for a time the magistrate of the nearby port city of Youghal. Raleigh didn't actually live at the castle, preferring the coastal views of Youghal, which in the 1960's served as the location for the seafaring classic film version of "Moby Dick". When Raleigh was locked in the Tower of London by Queen Elizabeth, he sold his Irish properties to Richard Boyle, the first Earl of Cork. The medieval castle of Lismore was heavily damaged during the English Civil War.

In 1753, the Castle and its lands passed into the hands of the William Cavendish, the 4th Duke of Devonshire. His grandson, the

6th Duke, William Spenser Cavendish, a patron of authors like Charles Dickens and William Makepeace Thakeray, began an extensive restoration of castle, taking shape as it is seen today. Joseph Paxton, designer of the Crystal Palace for the London Exhibition of 1851, originally came onto the Duke's estate as under-gardener, flourishing as a botanist, architect and engineer. As consultant and friend to the Duke, his influence shaped the present castle, with its added crenelated towers, mostly a Victorian era baronial mansion. The battlement walls surrounding the gardens, however, are the original medieval era fortification.

The most famous modern era resident of Lismore was Adele Astaire, the elder sister and first dancing partner of Fred Astair, who married the son of the 9th Duke of Devenshire, Charles Cavendish. She lived at the castle until his death in 1944 and later visited once a year. Fred Astaire also often stayed at the castle, writing at one point how many blankets he needed in the cold drafts of the place.

Lismore Castle is still the private home of the Devonshires, principally the younger generation, Lord and Lady Burlington. The castle interior is generally not open to visitors, though it is available for luxury rental accommodtaion when the owners are away. Hired for the full 13 rooms of the mansion, if you happen to have a handy €30,000 by the week. Lismore Castle is popular as a estate getaway for family reunions and weddings. For casual visitors to Lismore, it is the magnificent gardens which are open to the public.

The Lismore Castle Gardens on seven acres are divided into the Upper Garden, with the 17th century walled garden first constructed by Richard Boyle, the 1st Earl of Cork in 1605. The formal form of the garden of multiple levels and long rows of plantings remains much as it was 400 years ago, though the plants have changed somewhat to the taste of the current owners, and several contemporary sculptures have been added. The Lower Garden is more casual informal English garden style representing the 19th Century, an addition and expansion for the 6th Duke of Devonshire, designed under the guidance of Joseph Paxton. The gardens frame spectacular views of the castle and the surrounding countryside. The castle also has a small art gallery, the Lismore Castle Arts Gallery, added in 2003 to the west wing of the castle, which features changing exhibitions of contemporary art, workshops and art events.

In the lower grounds is the primeaval Yew Tree Walk, a canopy of the great ageless red-berried trees which predate the Victorian gardens. Sir Walter Raleigh's friend, the Elizabethan poet, Edmund Spencer, is said to have written "The Faerie Queen" sitting under the Yew tress still remaining at Lismore. You're surely unlikely to find any fairies still around, but you might encounter a curious piece of statuary along the path.

The Lismore Castle Gardens are open from 11am. to 4:45 pm every day from the 17th of March until September 30th. The art gallery is included with the gardens admission. Entrance is through the twin towered gatehouse. Lismore Castle is about 40 minutes from Cork and 20 from Dungarvan or Youghal. The historic heritage town of Lismore is a 10 minute stroll from the castle gates. The view from the little bridge to the east of the castle gate is one of the best castle views for shapshots, but beware the narrow walking lane of traffic.

BUNRATTY CASTLE
& FOLK PARK

Medieval Life and Times in County Clare

Bunratty Castle is one of the best pre-served single square castle keep in Ire-land, dating from around 1425. The castle was a stronghold of the O'Brien clan, later the Earls of Thomond and North Munster who ruled much of western Ireland. The main block of the castle which faces the road to Limerick from Shannon consists of three floors, each of a single great hall with narrow spiral stairs in the corners, now used for one way up and another way down, with the visitors to this very popu-lar attraction squeezing in the tight con-fines. The castle was restored in 1954 and decorated with original 15th and 16th Cen-tury furniture to represent the time when the Great Earl would have held court.

A wooden stairway has replaced what would have once been a drawbridge. The main Guard Hall on the entrance floor is used for the famous Bunratty Medieval Banquets, held twice nightly throughout the year. Above, is the Great Hall where the Earls of Thomond might have handed out weighty judgments of medieval law. A standard displays the family's coat of arms amidst the French and Flemish tapestries. On the highest floors, as was common in medieval keep construction, are the lord's chambers. The North Solar is perhaps the most interesting room with original wood paneling from the 1400's, lamps in the form of mythical creatures,

and an ornate table said to have been salvaged from the wreck of a ship-of-the-line of the Spanish Armada which met its disastrous fate on the rocky shoals off Northern Ireland.

Folk Park

The Folk Park at Bunratty Castle is a collection of about 30 buildings in the form of a complete village as it might have existed a hundred years ago, with structures from late medieval through Georgian and Victorian eras in a living reconstruction of the environment of rural Ireland, in a sense a medieval theme park without the rides, but with a real history.. A central village street is complete with printworks, schoolhouse, blacksmith, grocer and hardware, with houses

located among the green tree shrouded walks from farmhouses, to a fisherman's house from North Kerry, and the modest mansions of minor 19th Century gentry. The Bunratty Corn Barn, once a farmyard building is now the venue for the Bunratty Irish Nights, a rousing entertainment of Irish dance and music complimented by a family style dinner of home cooked Irish food and wine. The Irish Nights are held April to October. If you can make it to the castle events, local musicians also drop in to the pub at the park's

MacNamara's Hotel and Bar pub. The hotel is only a part of the folk park's village with no rooms, but the bar is fully licensed and can be entered from the street after hours. Or next door is Bunratty's Durty Nellys, a landmark village pub since 1620.

Entrance to Bunratty Castle is only with admission through the Folk Park. Reservation for seating tickets at the Bunratty Medieval Banquets with players in period costumes and more music and merriment or the Irish Dance Nights need to be arranged at the reception desk in the folk park entrance building or can be made online. If only in the area for a sort time reservations should be made in advance, especially in busy summer months. The castle's last entrance is at 4pm.

Though the Folk Park's MacNamara Hotel is only for display, the Bunratty Castle Hotel and Spa, an entirely separate property of upscale comfort is located directly across the Bunratty Green from the castle, next to the tourist friendly Creamery Bar pub and restaurant, a former dairy now a popular halfway rest stop from Galway to Kerry. Also on the Bunratty Green across from the castle is the Blarney Woolen Mills outlet center. For an even more luxurious stay with the flavor of noble's lifestyle nearby, Dromoland Castle Hotel is fifteen minutes to the west of Bunratty, with more O'Brien history. Bunratty Castle and Folk Park is only 5 miles from Shannon Airport and 8 miles east of Limerick.

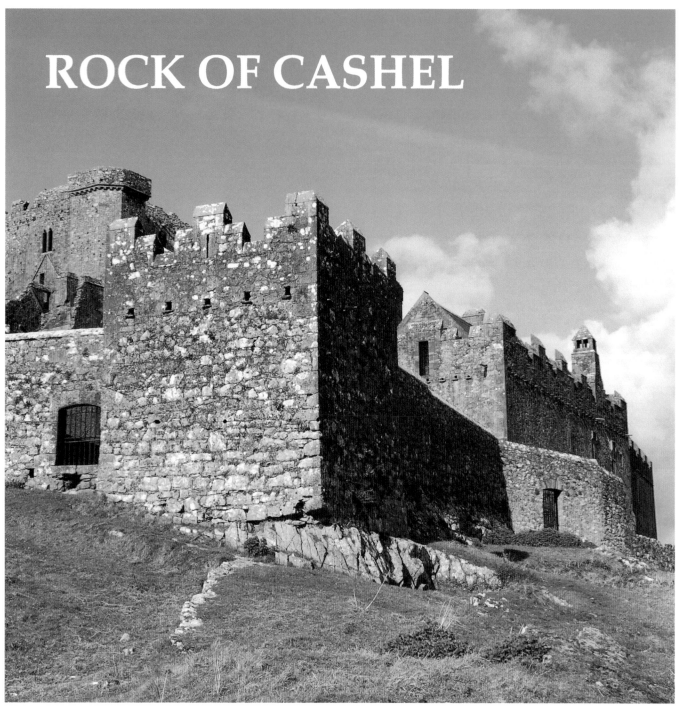

ROCK OF CASHEL

Saint Patrick's Rock Near Tipperary

Approaching from afar, the Rock of Cashel appears like an impregnable mystical fortress city, resting atop its singular hill like a sentinel, almost an island of land. Majestic and foreboding at the same time, this was a fortified medieval monastic city behind great walls rather than a castle, with most of its ruined buildings from the 12th and 13th Century when the fortress was granted to the Catholic Church.

The site of Cashel was the traditional seat of the Kings of Munster in Ireland since the 5th Century when St Patrick converted King Aenghus to Christianity, giving it the nickname of "St Patrick's Rock". Brian Boru was also crowned King of Ireland on this spot 500 years later in the 11th Century. You can see why this was a prime site for the seat of medieval power when standing at the foot of the great stones, the view from the Rock of Cashel looks out on all sides over miles of green fields of grazing sheep.

The buildings at the Rock of Cashel consist of the well preserved round tower, the earliest structure from 1100, a Romanesque royal chapel of King Cormac III of Munster, completed in 1134, with its twin towers and barrel vaulted roof and well-preserved 12th Century Irish fresco. The Cathedral at Cashel is the largest structure, completed in 1270, now roofless, with the sky showing through the great stone walls. The cathedral is connected to the residential quarters of the Bishops, with the Vicars Choral Hall added in the 15th Century. The Rock of Cashel was sacked and much of the complex destroyed by Cromwell's Parliamentary forces in 1647, when the Irish confederate troops defending the rock and all the Catholic priests were massacred, and many of its early religious artifacts looted.

Aside from the Rock of Cashel, the town of Cashel has a quarter of Georgian townhouses with the Bolton

Library housed in the Chapter House of the Cathedral Church of St. Patrick's Rock, containing one of the best antiquarian book collections outside of Dublin, assembled by Theophilis Bolton, the Archbishop of Cashel from 1730 to 1744, including works by Dante, Swift, Calvin, and Machiavelli, and the smallest book in Ireland. At the base of the Rock of Cashel, Brú Ború is a cultural historical village, celebrating native Irish music, song, dance and the-

atre, with a genealogy center for ancestry research. The 'Sounds of History' is an underground sonic journey through the story of Ireland from ancient times to the present day.

Starting from the castle rock, take a walk on the Tipperary Heritage Trail to two nearby abbey ruins, also destroyed in the English reformation. Hore Abbey, sometimes known as St.Mary's, a ruined Cistercian monastery previously belonging to the Benedictines, but given over to the more powerful order in 1270, and Dominic's Abbey to the southeast of the Rock of Cashel, founded in 1243 by Dominican friar David McKelly, later Archbishop of Cashel who is buried in the Chapel of the Apostles within the walls of "The Rock".

Cashel in Tipperary County is one of the most visited tourist destinations in southwest Ireland, two hours from Dublin via the M8 motorway, about an hour from Limerick or Cork. Opening hours vary depending on season, closing at 7pm in summer and 5:30pm most of the rest of the year, but last entrance is 45 minutes before closing.

TRIM CASTLE

Ireland's Largest Anglo-Norman Castle

The first Plantagenet king, Henry II, was a shrewd fellow, in a constant chess-game of consolidating his power over his Anglo-Norman empire, from the French domains of Aquitaine, Anjou and Normandy, to the Scottish border, to which in 1172 he added Ireland. Shortly after his arrival in Dublin, and declaring himself Lord of Ireland, King Henry granted Hugh De Lacy the lordship of the kingdom of Meath (now just County Meath), covering the land to the northwest of Dublin. King Henry feared a challenge from Richard de Clare, the famous "Strongbow", the 2nd Earl of Pembroke, who had come from Wales two years before, supporting the dispossessed King of Leinster in the southeast of the island. Hugh De Lacy selected the village of Trim to build a castle on the site of an earlier wooden ring fort, along the meandering Boyne River. King Henry later undercut Strongbow's potential to challenge him by encouraging the marriage of the very loyal knight William Marshal to de Clare's daughter, and installing him as the Earl of Pembroke, over de Clare.

Trim Castle remains as the largest and one of the best preserved of the Norman age castles in Ireland - though preserved is a relative term. The first wooden fort was fortified as a stone fortress after being attacked by the last Gaelic High King of Ireland, Rory O'Connor. The current castle of high stone curtain walls surrounding a single inner stone keep was formed over a period of 30 years, begun under Hugh de Lacy and continued by his son Walter who succeeded him in 1186. The most distinctive feature of Trim Castle is its unique twenty-sided high

17

keep, laid out in a cross shape. As an early castle of its kind, there is no inner bailey wall, but the keep stands on its own, protected by a complex gate and bridge tower, similar to Bunratty in the west, the foundations of which remain. Much of the outer curtain walls are intact, once surrounded by a moat, though now a mostly dry gassy flatland floodplain bristling with gorse.

Only the foundations are left of the castle's Great Hall and other residential buildings of the medieval age, built not in the keep but against the walls, found next to the distinctive below ground stone tunnel to the River Gate, where goods could be delivered to the fortress by a canal. Trim Castle was not a

residence castle in later ages like others, disused mostly by the end of the 15th Century, so remains laid out mostly as it was in the era of the de Lacys, and so representative of the period that it served as the movie location stand-in for York Castle in the Mel Gibson movie "Braveheart". A film about the history of the castle and its preservation reconstruction is presented in the visitor center along with artifacts and exhibits of the past of the region and a souvenir shop.

The medieval town of Trim is about 40 minutes drive from Dublin Airport. The castle stands right at the edge of town, flanked by the main road with a city parking lot facing the main entrance gate. Trim Castle is open daily from April through October, and weekends only from November to Easter. Admission to Trim Castle includes a guided tour of the castle keep. From the castle, stroll the paths of the Boyne River flood plain or venture to the medieval town across the "Millennium Bridge", a wooden foot bridge

across the stream which gets its name from when they built it during the castle's restoration in 2000. There is a Failte Ireland tourist office around the corner from the castle entrance with a café. Trim Castle is one of the most visited of its kind in Ireland and can get very busy in summer months.

The village of Trim itself, a designated heritage town which gets its name from the Gaelic for "Ford of the Elder Trees" is in an area surrounded by the most medieval buildings and ancient sites in Ireland. Within 15 to 30 minutes by car are the abbey ruins of the Priory of St John the Baptist and the Bective Abbey, the Celtic fort site of The Hill of Tara, the Battle of the Boyne museum and the prehistoric megalithic site of Newgrange and Bru Na Boinne. There are a number of hotels, guest houses around Trim, with the elegant modern Trim Castle Hotel directly across the street, cozy historic Highfield House guest house with a view of the castle, or for the more luxury minded the new Knightsbrook Hotel & Golf Resort is 5 minutes away.

DUNLUCE CASTLE

Dramatic Coastal Ruins of Antrim

Dunluce Castle stands on a tower of black basalt, 90 feet above the roiling sea below, with ruined jagged walls like a ghostly inhabitant of a Gothic thriller, or a smugglers' sea adventure. Located along the Antrim Coast drive between the village of Bushmills, known for its Irish Whiskey distillery and the famed Royal Portrush Golf Course, the castle ruin, perched on its spear of land has been the subject of many a painter, especially for its most dramatic outline above the cliffs from the eastern approach.

The earliest medieval fortress on the spot was most likely built be Richard De Burgh under the Anglo-Norman rule of Ireland, though some defense probably occupied it since Celtic times. The outer castle walls of the current castle date back to the 14th Century and the time of the MacQuillans, who controlled the trade routes along the North Antrim coast between the Bann and Bush Rivers. Most of the remains of the castle buildings as seen today are from 16th and 17th Centuries when the north coast of

Ulster was in the hands of the MacDonnells. The MacDonnells were an offshoot of the Scottish clan of the McDonalds, known as the Lords of the Isles, that part of Scotland closest to the coast of Northern Ireland. The headlands of Scotland are so close to the Irish shore it raised the legend of Finn MacCool and the nearby Giant's Causeway.

MacCool was a giant married to a woman with a good deal more sense than he. He could see the shoreline of his enemy giant, Banandonner, in Scotland across the sea and built a causeway across the water to take him on, only to discover that the Scotish giant was much larger than his distant view had suggested. Finn McCool ran home to his wife, Oonagh, beside himself what to do. His clever wife had the idea to disguise her husband as a baby and put him in a hastily made cradle. When Benandonner came a-pounding on the door, she invited him in for tea. On seeing how large was the infant, and imagining how huge a giant the father must be, the Scottish Giant now ran home and ripped up the causeway after himself, to keep Finn MacCool from following him.

Dunluce Castle changed hands a number of times among the fighting family, principally symbolized by the rowdy and wild, Sorley Boy MacDonnell. In 1584, Sir John Perrot, the Lord Deputy of Ireland, raided the castle, which he took easily because he had brought three cannons, against which the old stonework castle walls could not defend. Two years later, Queen Elizabeth returned the castle to the family. When the Spanish Armada ship-of-the-line, the Girona, ran aground on the nearby rocks, Sorley Boy was able to salvage three of his own cannons from the ship wreck.

When James VI of Scotland became James I of England, the MacDonnells were favored loyal kinsmen and granted the lands of the Glens and coast of Antrim. In 1620, the English king required all his earls in Ulster to build a castle on their baronies and Sir Randal MacDonnell set about to improve and expand Dunluce Castle with the addition of a new manor house and quarters, but it was only a few short years before misfortune fell. Part of the lower kitchens cascaded into the sea one night in 1639 during a grand dinner party, and in 1651, the belongings of the family were seized by agents of Oliver Cromwell. The family went into exile during the Cromwellian years and after the Restoration, virtually abandoned the castle. The castle was granted to the Northern Ireland government in 1928.

The castle can only be reached across a bridge from the mainland courtyard and visitors center. A 10 minute film about the castle's history begins a visit. Originally, the bridge was a

rickety wooden structure which could be broken under attack, making the castle nearly impregnable during the Middle-Ages. Later the crossing of the rocky 30 meter deep gap was supported by a stone arch. The oldest parts of the castle defenses are the outer wall and two round towers, with the Scottish-style gatehouse added a bit later. The row of columns running parallel to the east gate is known as a Loggia, framing a formal garden from the Elizabethan era. The rest of the roofless building walls remaining are from the 1600's, including a Great Hall with two fireplaces and three bow windows, a pantry, buttery and kitchen with a huge fireplace. A manmade tunnel running under the north east tower, opening out onto the cliff, dates back a thousand years to the earliest structure on the site. Back across the bridge on the sloping landward approach is where the 17th Century visitors' lodgings, stables and the Earl's gardens stood.

The castle is open daily all year, from April to September 10am to 6pm, and October to March 10am to 5pm. Last admission is a half-hour before closing. Guided tours are available with advance booking. When the castle is closed, you can walk down the steps, past the wishing well and mermaid's cave to the coastal rocks. The ruins of St. Cuthbert's Church are a short walk from the castle grounds on the small road opposite the Portrush entrance to the castle.

KING JOHN'S CASTLE

Lackland's Fortress in Limerick

You own it, you name it. While King John's Castle is in Limerick, in the heart of Ireland, King John never set foot in the medieval fortress that bears his name. The Vikings had built a fort on a flat island in a split in the Shannon River, from which they raided and dominated the region in near constant conflict with the Irish clans of Munster. The Normans from England came to Ireland in the 12th Century under Henry II, who had built an empire including half of France, and intent on adding Ireland. Donal Mór O'Brien, the Irish King of Thomond, controlling what is now most of County Clare and southwest Ireland, submitted to Henry at Cashel in 1172, retaining his position and holding back Norman encroachment until his death in 1194, when Henry named his youngest son, John, as Lord of Ireland.

King John had such a bad reputation as a wastrel and military failure, that no other English kings were ever named John. After his brother Richard I, popularly known as "Lionheart" died, many of the lords of France who had been subdued by his father Henry and feared his brother, wouldn't swear fealty to John, losing the imperial lands in France and giving him the

popular name in England of John "Lackland". King John's oppressive tax policies brought down the wrath of the English barons and he was forced to sign the Magna Carta at Runnymede in 1215. He died a year later from a fever caught with his army in East Anglia while trying to regain the power he'd signed away, leaving his kingdom torn by civil war.

King John's Castle, a 13th Century Anglo-Norman fortress built between 1200 and 1210 located in the center of Limerick on "King's Island" with the waters of the River Shannon lapping at its stone foundations, was a pioneer of castle construction in its day with several of its innovations seen in the great "Iron Ring" castles of Edward I in Wales. King John's Castle retains many of the features which made it unique for its day, with its impressive gate house of high narrow semi-circular stone

towers protecting the approach from the river, which once housed the portcullis system. The battlements and corner towers can be climbed for panoramic views of the River Shannon flowing under the arched Thomand Bridge and surrounding countryside.

The Castle has recently been updated with a new visitor experience with interactive exhibitions, computer animations and multi-media presentations to bring the castle's history to life. A hands-on history approach offers a chance for kids to play dress-up in medieval garb and relive the past recreated in a medieval campaign tent in the courtyard, including a blacksmith's forge and scenes of a 17th Century siege with guides in period costume. Outside, archeological excavations of the 13th century undercroft of the officers' quarters uncovered in 1995 are open to view in the courtyard surrounded by demonstrations of medieval crafts. In one complex of passages in the thick walls is a replica of what would have been the mint where the king's coins would have been made. In another chamber, a rather fanciful mannequin likeness of King John seems to fascinate kids with its image of a medieval king on his throne while a recorded presentation tells his story, though no-one really knows what King John looked like. There are a few medieval and

later representations of him, but none were from life. The effigy on his tomb in Worchester Cathedral was done 15 years after his death. What is known about his physical person is that he was 5'5" tall, the shortest of his kin, so Claude Raines in the 1940's movie version of "Robin Hood" might have been close enough. King John was a restless monach who spent much of his reign moving from one castle to another among the royal hunting forests, which is from where some of the connection to the Robin Hood legend comes. He came to Ireland once as King in 1210, landing at Waterford, touring Dublin, Meath and the North of Ireland, but not Limerick where the castle named for him was being completed.

In the middle ages, the settlement on King's Island was known as "England Town" while across the river beyond the protective walls and gate house of the castle was "Irish Town". The castle was heavily damaged in the Cromwellian Siege of Limerick in 1642, the first of five sieges of the city during the Irish Rebellion in the 17th century, with only part of its full original form remaining. The current entrance to King Johns Castle is through the modern vistors center on the cobbled walk through Limerick's Medieval Heritage district which stretches between King

John's castle and the Hunt Museum across the bridge from Merchant's Quay. The heritage area is still recovering from years of blight which the city suffered the late 20th Century, but you'll find the pedestrian zone with many of Limerick's busy bars and restaurants across the quay.

King Johns Castle in Limerick is open daily all year from 10:30-4:30 November to March and 10-5:30 April to October. There is a car park in the summer and street parking available nearby.

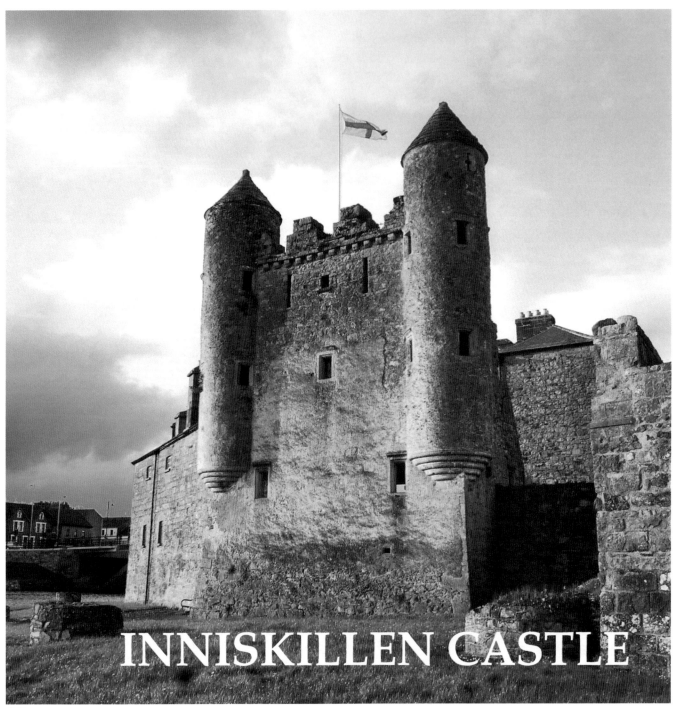

INNISKILLEN CASTLE

North Ireland Conflict History in Fermanagh

Enniskillen in Fermanaugh County has played a most significant part in the story of Northern Ireland. The location was first established as a strategic stronghold of the Gaelic Maguire clan on an island formed from the river waters passing between the two main bodies of Upper and Lower Lough Erne, the lakes of many islands formed by the River Erne. The original stone castle, a square tower house built in the 1400's by Hugh Maguire "the Hospitable" to guard the few passes into Fermanagh from attack by the O'Rourke and O'Donnell clans to the south and west, replaced an earler earthen fort, parts of which can still be seen in the moatwork along the lake shore. Maquire's castle was expanded in 1580 with the addition of the Watergate tower, which is now the most recognizable feature of the castle structure with its twin towers overlooking the waters of the River Erne, which have receded over time away from the gate, forming a flood plain where luxury cruise boats motor past in the channel.

Beginning with a strategic campaign of the British in 1594 to control the northern province of Ulster, the English under a Captain McDowel captured the castle, which was then recaptured by Connacht Maguire and eventually retaken by the British in 1607. The Protestant English King James I, from whom we get the King James Bible, taking the throne after his cousin Queen Elizabeth, declared the Earls of Ulster as traitors and seized their land. The king appointed William Cole to establish an English settlement at Enniskillen, beginning what is known as the Plantation of Ulster, when the lands of the native Irish lords and farmers were seized and granted to planters who would be loyal to the Protestant English crown, many coming from Scotland and northern England, which is why today Northern Ireland is part of the United Kingdom, and the source of 400 years of conflict between Protestants and Catholics. Enniskillen is important in the Northern Ireland story as both where the conflict known as the "troubles" began, and where on November 8th, 1987, the explosion of an IRA bomb during a WWI Remembrance Day ceremony, which killed 11 and wounded another 64, turned the tide toward peace. The bomb, planted behind the wall of a pub across from the Enniskillen War Memorial, was intended as an attack on British Soldiers, but 10 of the killed were civilians and many of the wounded were children, which horrified both sides to say "enough", eventually leading to the current state of reconciliation. Today, the casual tourist will hardly notice any of the past conflict, though small birds on the rebuilt War Memorial commemorate the victims of the bomb and hope for continued peace.

In 1611, William Cole had the entire town of Enniskillen rebuilt to his specifications and much of it remains according to his plans, though traffic through town can get very congested at times due to its old layout. By 1689 the town had grown significantly and during the arising of renewed conflict from the ousting of Catholic King James II by his Protestant rival, William III, Enniskillen and Derry were the focus of the Williamite resistance in Ireland. For much of its history, Enniskillen Castle has been the regimental station of the British Royal Dragoons and Fusiliers.

Inniskillings Regimental Museum

The square keep of Enniskillen Castle houses a museum of the Royal Inniskilling Fusiliers and 6th Dragoon Guards of the British Army "The Inniskillings" (from where the town gets its name or vice versa), with displays of weapons and vehicles along with uniforms and medals of the regiments. The castle also houses the Fermanagh County Museum. Behind the keep, overlooking the River Erne is the regimental firing

range where bullets would be fired into sand bags on the wall to capture bullets from flying into the countryside, but the sound would resonate in an intimating raucous of regularity in more tense times. Check out the German Mortar captured in WWI and dedicated to the bravery of one Lieutenant J. A. O. Brook. One of several free public car parks for Enniskillen is directly next to the castle along the river front. The castle and museums are open all year 2pm to 5pm on Mondays and Saturdays, 10am to 5pm

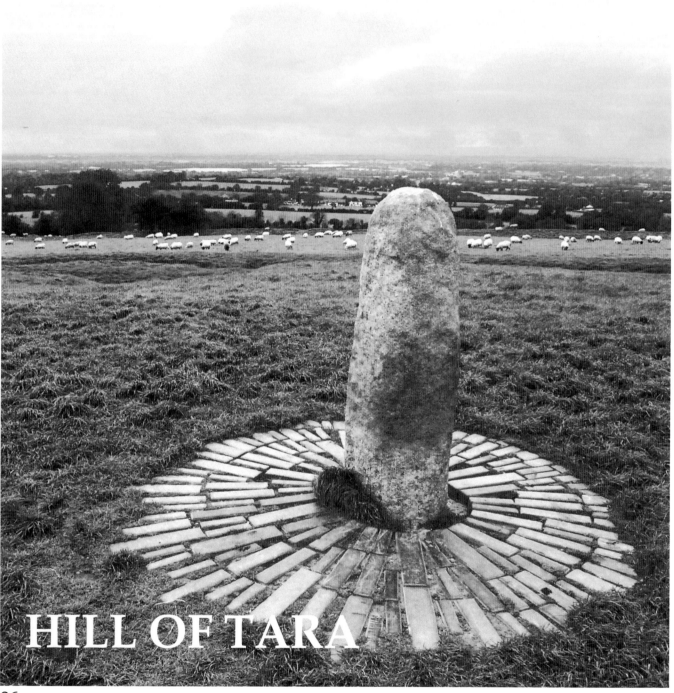

HILL OF TARA

Ireland's Sacred Sanctuary of the High Kings

William Butler Yeats called it "the most consecrated spot in Ireland". In 1843 almost a million people gathered on the rolling grassy knoll to listen to Daniel O'Connell "The Liberator" speak out for Irish independence from Great Britain. It was once even believed that the Ark of the Covenant was buried here. The Hill of Tara is an undulating low-lying ridge overlooking the Meath valley, with its grass covered hill revealing forms of an ancient fortified center for druidic and Celtic culture in Ireland. Before Christianty and after, the site was the where the Celtic High Kings of Ireland were invested. According to tradition, when a true Irish or Scottish King placed his foot on the Stone of Destiny, it cried out to confirm his rightful reign.

The Hill of Tara was the royal center of Mide – the Middle Kingdom of the Irish island, which incorporated modern Meath, Cavan and Longford counties. The name Tara comes from Teamhair na Ri meaning Sanctuary of the Kings and it is said almost a quarter of Ireland can be seen from its hilltop, though that would require a really clear day and mythic eyesight. Whatever structures may have been present in ancient times are no longer in evidence on the Tara hill. There are no great stones like Stonehenge, but the remains of earthen work defensive channels, carved into the hill. The oldest visible monument is the passage tomb of Dumha na nGiall, dating back to about 3,000 B.C. But Tara gained its greatest importance in the Iron Age of 600 BC to 400 AD, and less so into the early Christian period, when monastic monks with their abbeys superseded the Earth gods and goddesses. The stones on the site today are modern replacements representing the originals.

A statue of St Patrick stands at the edge of the monument - perhaps a stick in the eye to the Druids and the old faiths. According to the legend, in 433, as the Druid tribes prepared to celebrate the Feast of Tara at the spring equinox, St Patrick lit a Paschal Fire on the nearby Hill of Slane to celebrate Easter in direct defiance of the earlier pagan ritual. The fire could be seen from Tara and the Druids demanded that King Laoghaire have the fire extinguished that night, lest it burn forever. The outraged king led his Druids to challenge St Patrick and his new mono God with their earth magic, but couldn't defeat him, and eventually the king and his followers converted to Christianity.

The most interesting monument still at the site is the Lia Fail – the Stone of Destiny, the standing stone located in the Forrad – the Royal Seat. The stone hasn't shouted out for a new king in a thousand years, but from the dark marks of hands on it, a few have tried for the post. Also still visible and labeled with signs are the so-called Banqueting Hall, The Fort of Kings, The Mound of Hostages, Cormac's House, the Sloping Trenches and The Rath of the Synods – the supposed hiding place of the covenant, though now it mostly hides a bit of careless debris behind a locked steel bar gate. The Hill of Tara was finally abandoned by Mael Sechlainn, the High King of Ireland in 1022, leaving the region to the battles of the middle-ages, and Catholic and Protestant conflicts in the surrounding Boyne Valley.

The Hill of Tara is a mystical place and the most sacred site in Ireland, but is mostly a walk among the hills with curiosity of what took place there. A church and graveyard stand next to the open forms on the hill. The site of the Hill of Tara itself is open all year round and is free to enter. In fact, there are no real gates or fences, not even to keep out the sheep who keep the grass shorn. The Visitor Center located inside the church offers an audio-visual presentation, guided tours and audio guides is open from mid-May to mid-September. There is a café and souvenir bookshop, Maguires nearby, as well as some craft shops next to the site.

To get to the Hill of Tara requires a car, along some back roads through County Meath, though many bus tours available from Dublin stop there. Other sights to visit near The Hill of Tara are the megalith monuments of the World Heritage site of Newgrange and Bu na Boinne, Trim Castle, the largest Norman era castle, Kells (from where the Book of Kells came), the medieval walled town of Drogheda, and the site of the Battle of the Boyne.

BELLE ISLE ESTATE

Castle and Lodgings on Lough Erne "A World Away"

Ducks paddling on the quiet still waters, only disturbed by the cast of a fishing line into the lake, make the Belle Isle Estate seem like another world. Intellectually, you know you're in the modern world, but crossing the bridge from the mainland onto one of the eight flat and lush picturesque islands among gentle hills on the northern tip of Upper Lough Erne, the delta like river system which surrounds Enniskillen in County Fermanagh, feels as if lost in time, where the name, meaning beautiful island, fits well.

At the heart of the estate is Belle Isle Castle, a 17th Century manor currently owned by the Duke of Abercorn who took pride in creating his oasis in such an unspoilt landscape. Belle Isle was for centuries only reachable by boat, which kept it pristine and remote. After the establishment of the plantations in Ulster, the lands of Belle Isle were granted to an English soldier, Sir Ralph Gore, following what was known as the "Flight of the Earls" in 1607. The oldest part of

the house, the Hamilton Wing was built in 1680 with the rest of the castle expanded in the 1700's with addition of the walled gardens, and added to again in 1850. A bridge to the island was finally built in 1880. The entrance to the castle is through an impressive double-vaulted chamber, leading to the elegant drawing room with a magnificent marble fireplace, decorated with English antiques and Russian paintings from St Petersburg. From the other end of the entrance hall one finds the Grand Hall, an imposing banqueting room with a Minstrel's Gallery above and rich red color scheme to compliment the Victorian art.

A variety of accommodations are available at Belle Isle. Visitors to the estate can stay in one of the eight bedrooms in the manor house, each with antique furnishings, some with oak beams and four poster beds. The castle can accommodate up to fourteen guests for the weddings for which the estate is well known. If lodging in the castle itself is not in the scheme, Belle Isle Estate offers eight self-catering apartments in the Courtyard, a listed former stables complex added to the property in 1860. Each apartment has its own character and sleeping options ranging from singles to family apartments for up to six. The courtyard apartments are at ground level, with some outfitted for the disabled and some with children's lofts. The 150 year old Coach House has been converted into two substantial home-like apartments with living room, kitchen, dining area and log stove and bedrooms for up to four. Set away from the main mansion, the Bridge House sits at the edge of the water surrounded by woodlands with its own boat mooring, while Cathcart's Lodge is a two bedroom bungalow on the opposite side of the water close to the fishing stands.

Belle Isle is the perfect spot if all you want to do is sit all day with a fishing line in the reeds and forget the stress of the world, but for those who need activity, the environs of surrounding Fermanagh offers lots to discover. Located at the castle is the Belle Isle School of Cookery, offering cooking classes from one day courses to a full week of gourmet cuisine lessons and experimentation in a fully outfitted kitchen. But beware, you'll be forced to eat your own cooking at the end of the course, so learn well. There are a number of walks and rambles through the islands and country side surrounding the Bell Isle Estate. Boat cruises exploring Lough Erne are available at Enniskillen. Eight golf courses lie within 30 miles, including the stunning Lough Erne Golf Resort with its new Nick Faldo course. The National Trust Houses of Florence Court and Castle Coole are within 15 minutes, or explore the underground deep caverns of the Marble Arch Caves Geopark. The Ulster American Folk Park nearby in Omagh is definitely worth a visit for Scots-Irish heritage and history. In late autumn, the weather can turn to a bit of a chill and gloom, but from the end of October to January its hunting season at Belle Isle with packages for Woodcock and Snipe available in the Hamilton Wing for groups. Non-UK Residents require a £12 license. Belle Isle is about a 20 minute drive from Enniskillen, 2 hours from Belfast and three hours from Dublin.

DROMOLAND CASTLE
HOTEL & GOLF

Live Like An Irish Legend

If you've envisioned living like a royal in an Ireland castle estate, Dromoland Castle gloriously fits the bill. It is the historic seat of Ireland's O'Brien Clan, ancestral home of the Barons of Inchiquin, direct Gaelic descendants of Brian Boru, the High King of Ireland from the 11th century. The Dromoland Estate came into being in the 1500's. The current Dromoland Castle is a gothic revival manor, redesigned in 1835 from the original 16th Century Renaissance residence, which in turn replaced a former early fortified castle. Its blue limestone with turrets set in a verdant park of the former estate desmesne make for the romantic image of a true baronial manor. Perched on a sloping hill above the lake around which the long entrance drive winds through the grounds, the castle was refurbished and transformed into a luxury hotel in 1962, and since recognized as one of Ireland's most splendid castle estate hotels.

The country club styled 410-acres of the estate retain the feeling of a noble life-style, ducks and other feathery water creatures roam the grassy grounds attracted by the glassy beautiful lake of water lillies, surrounded by a championship golf course. The interior of the Dromoland Castle Hotel features magnificent wood and stone carvings, hand-carved paneling, original oil paintings, oriental carpets, damask window draperies, and Irish heirloom antique furnishings. The hotel consists of 85 guestrooms and 13 deluxe suites and staterooms individually designed and decorated by designer Carol Roberts of Bath, England. The suites at Dromoland offer the feeling of truly living like a peer, high arching ceilings and old world elegance, massive marble bathrooms, all you can expect from an estate hotel. A few nights in the Queen Anne Suite will have you convinced you've been anointed a baronet. Guests of the Dromoland Castle Hotel can hunt or fish in the estate lake,

well stocked with trout and perch, play tennis on the estate's two all-weather courts, golf, ride horseback at the neighboring Equestrian Center, cycle the surrounding countryside, enjoy archery or clay shooting, biking, or just roam the beautiful grounds of Irish green in a horse drawn carriage.

Dromoland Castle's estate features a private championship 18-hole, par-72 golf course designed by Ron Kirby and JB Carr, which has hosted a number of professional and pro-

celebrity competitions. Dromoland Castle's golf course is complemented by a unique practice facility, which has 10 driving days fully automated with "power tees" and putting greens. The Bunker and Chipping Green offer a variety of lies, slopes and grass lengths to practice from, including a riveted face style bunker modeled on the famous 'Road Hole' bunker on the 17th at St Andrews. The clubhouse also provides computerized exercise equipment, sauna and steam room facilities and a 17-metre swimming pool.

The Spa at Dromoland, located within the castle walls, offers 6 treatment rooms, Relaxation room, Pedicure & Manicure booths, Hair Design Studio and an outdoor Hydro Pool with relaxation patio. The spa design soothes with an air of tranquility with light wood furniture, shades of beige, stone floors, and its own water wall.

Dromoland's Earl of Thomond Restaurant provides elegance and excellence offering the finest in French Provençale cuisine as well as traditional Irish specialties with fresh, locally procured ingredients. House specialties include fillet of Lamb with Foie Gras and roasted fillet of Turbot, studded with bay leaves, complimented with a special collection

of speciality wines. In addition to The Earl of Thomond Restaurant is the more casual Fig Tree Restaurant with a menu tailored to a more informal dining experience. Afternoon Tea is still a historic tradition at Dromoland, served from 3 to 5 in the castle's elegant Drawing Room where guests can sample teas, cakes and pastries, freshly made that day.

Dromoland Castle Hotel and Country Estate is a convenient 7 miles from Shannon International Airport, between Shannon and Limerick, and 10 minutes from the village of Bunratty with its family popular Bunratty Castle and Folk Park. Seasonal Packages are available.

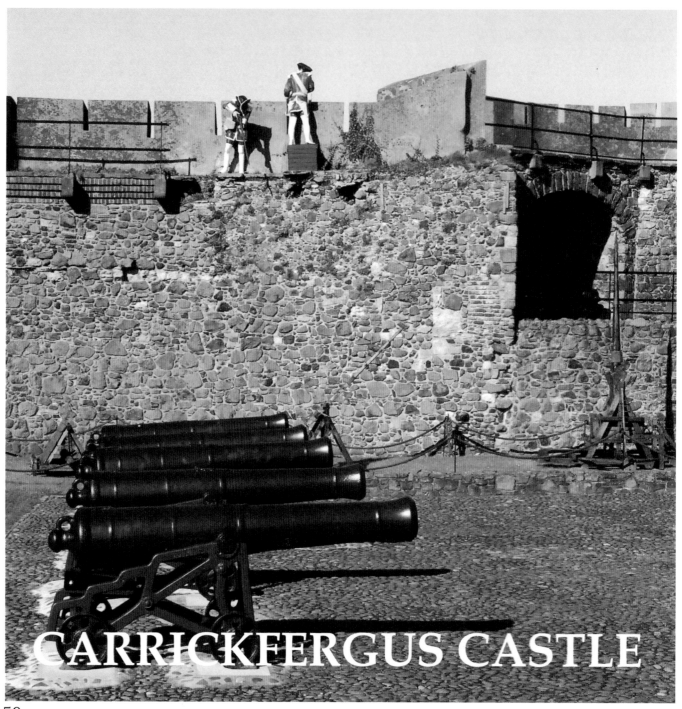

CARRICKFERGUS CASTLE

Guarding the Sea Approach on Antrim Coast

The castle at Carrickfergus is dramatically located at the entrance to the long bay which leads inland to Belfast, its strong stone walls once nearly surrounded by water, and has the distinction of being one of the most assaulted fortresses in Ireland. It has played a role in wars from the Norman conquest of Ireland at the end of the Viking age, an Irish revolt in the Elizabethan era, the Plantation of Ulster and Jacobite-Williamite War, the Napoleonic Wars, and even the American Revolution. One of the best preserved medieval constructions in the Irish Isle, the castle remained in use as a military outpost until the split of Northern Ireland and the Republic when it was turned over by the British Army in 1928 to become a historic monument to 800 years of conflict.

Carrickfergus Castle was first built as a fortress in the early days of the Norman conquest of Ireland. John de Courcy, a knight under the Plantagenet King Henry II marched north in 1176 to take the lands of Ulster, though without the permission of King Henry II.

De Courcy established the commanding site at Carrickfergus as his headquarters, beginning the fortress in 1177. De Courcy is responsible for building the inner ward, with a small bailey and the high curtain wall with the eastern gate. De Courcy allied himself through marriage to the Norse by marrying the daughter of King Godred Olofssen of the Isle of Mann. In 1205, under orders from King John, Hugh de Lacey the younger, the son of the Lord of Meath, was given the task to take the lands of Ulster which had been granted to the favored de Laceys. De Courcy was accounted to be a fierce warrior and said to sleep in his armor, but de Lacey succeeded in removing him, taking the castle while the erstwhile lord escaped to the sea. De Courcy tried to retake the castle with a force of Norwegian backed men from the Isle of Mann, but the attempt failed. The castle was re-enforced under de Lacey with expansion of the curtain wall to protect from the sea rocks. The features remaining from this period are the Romanesque window of a chapel, the ribbed vault over the entrance passage where a yeoman figure now stands guard, a "murder hole" and the massive portcullis protecting the massive gatehouse.

The other substantive features of the castle date from the 16th and 17th centuries, during the age of gunpowder. The castle and the surrounding countryside of present day County Antrim were the site of the Battle of Carrickfergus in 1597, an uprising of the Gaelic MacDonnell clan against the English forces of Queen Elizabeth I, and one hundred years later, the fight for control of the north of Ireland between the Catholic King James II who had been deposed by the

Protestant William of Orange. King William III landed in Ireland on the 14th of June 1690 after a successful siege of the castle by his German born commander, General Meinholt Schomberg and went on to end James' challenge for the crown at the Battle of the Boyne a month later. Improvements were made in this period to accommodate artillery, with gunports and embrasures added for cannons on the walls. The cannons are the most notable feature of the remaining historic

recreation at the castle. Victorian era living quarters and barracks had been added in the years since, but were removed after the 1930's to return the castle to its more medieval form.

Carrickfergus Castle also curiously played a small role in the American War for Independence. In 1778, Captain John Paul Jones on patrol off the North Ireland Coast with his 18 gun sloop, the Ranger, to harass British shipping, lured a Royal Navy ship-of-the-line, the HMS Drake, from the channel and engaged in an hour long battle in sight of the castle battlements. This was the second engagement between the two vessels. The English ship was captured and delivered to France in the first decisive campaign for fledgling the American Continental navy.

Carrickfergus Castle is about a 15 minute drive from downtown Belfast and the beginning of the Antrim Coast scenic driving route. The castle is open daily from 10am to 6pm April through September and 10am to 4 pm from October to March. Last admission is 30 minutes before closing.

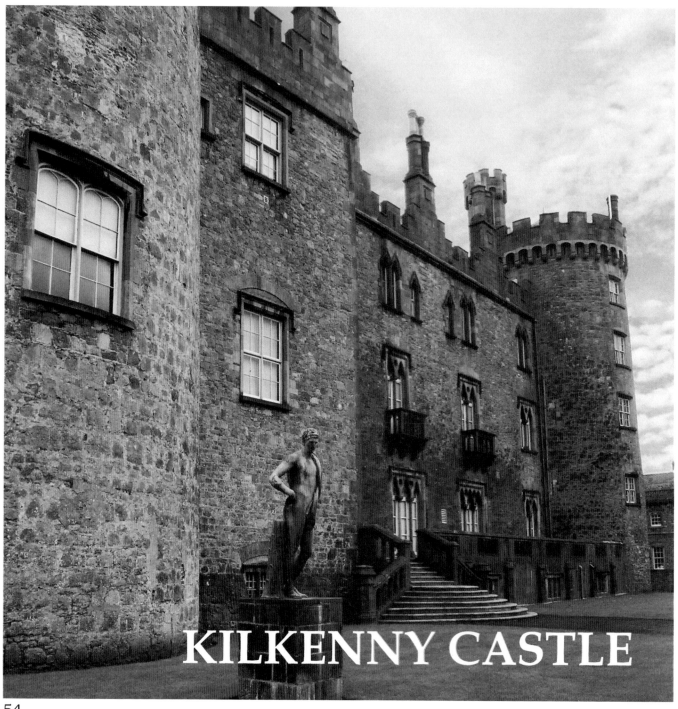

KILKENNY CASTLE

Norman Castle to Victorian Baronial Palace

One of Ireland's most important and most visited castles about an hour from Dublin sits on a crossing of the River Nore in the center of Kilkenny. The original dates for a first fortress on the spot vary, with likely an earlier home of the Irish Kings of Ossory and the Celts before them, but the first significant castle, likely of wood, was built by Richard de Clare "Strongbow" who first established the Anglo-Norman presence in Ireland in the 12th Century. William Marshal, the crusader hero under Henry II and protector of his son and later king, John, married Strongbow's daughter Isabel and succeeded to his father-in-law's lands in 1189. It was Marshal who built the square stone Norman castle, begun in 1195 and completed in 1213

Unlike Norman single keep castles like Bunratty, Kilkenny was constructed as a square of walls with four round corner towers, more akin to the fortress designs of the Welsh coast and at Roscommon, surrounded by a moat, which form the basis of the current castle, though much changed. Inside the walls originally were wooden constructed halls, living quarters and barracks. Unlike the other Norman castles in Ireland which decayed into ruin over time, Kilkenny remained a major residence and seat of wealth, and transformed over centuries into a castellated baronial manor house, with the castle defenses exchanged for parkland and

gardens. Three of the original towers remain, but much of the castle has been added to with later Victorian age remodeling.

A symbol of the Norman occupation and English power in Ireland, the castle was bought in 1391 by James Butler, 3rd Earl of Ormonde. The Butler family ruled the surrounding countryside for almost five hundred years, gaining significant land holdings with the dissolution of the monasteries by Henry VIII. Kilkenny Castle was the site of the meeting of the General Assembly of the Catholic Confederate goverment of Ireland in the 1640s, and suffered badly under siege by Cromwell's forces in 1650, during which one of the towers was destroyed.

It is claimed Kilkenny Castle is notoriously haunted, with ghosts supposedly not allowing anyone to sleep overnight in comfort in the last 150 years. One suspects there are likely other causes for that, but the castle did attract the interest of famed British occultist Aleister Crowley, who bought a part interest in the castle from the last Bulter when the family fell on hard times in the market crash of the 1930's. Details on ghosts at Kilkenny Castle are sparse; a "lady in white" seems to be occassionally spotted on the stairs and in the gardens. There is a local Ghost Walk Tour of Kilkenny town which gathers at the castle gates.

Kilkenny Castle was granted to a trust in 1968 and extensive refurbishments made. Most of the original Butler furnishings were sold off at auction in 1935, but some were re-acquired and added to by paintings from the Irish National Gallery. The castle and grounds are now managed by the OPW, with regular tours, and the gardens and parkland adjoining the castle open to the public. The Rose Garden on the city side of the castle is used as the location for weddings against the backdrop of the castle towers. The expansive green grass park extends from the eastern side along the river bank, and is popular for weekends.

Tours of the interior of the castle lead through a number of 17th to 19th century palace style rooms of rich furnishings and paintings. Portraits of the various Butlers are omni-present. The Blue Bedroom and Chinese Bedroom are of particular fascination, but perhaps the most impressive room is the Robertson Picture Galley. Designed by architect William Robertson in the early 1800's, where a wing was added to the castle over earlier foundations with a long picture gallery. A high arched ceiling with skylights was added later, giving the chamber a grand scale. The earlier medieval heritage life of the castle can be found in the undercroft of the west tower with a massive cirular chamber of thick 13th Century walls and arrow loops. In the Medieval Room of the south tower, visitors can view an audio visual presentaion of the history of the castle.

Kilkenny Castle is open for guided tours only, from October to March and April to May, daily from 10.30am to 5pm (though closed for lunch from 12.45 to 2.00pm). From June to August, tours are offered from 9.30am to 7.pm and in September from 10am to 6.30pm. The exterior grounds are open without charge. Tours take about an hour. Kilkenny Castle is a very popular tourist spot and waits can get long in the summer months.

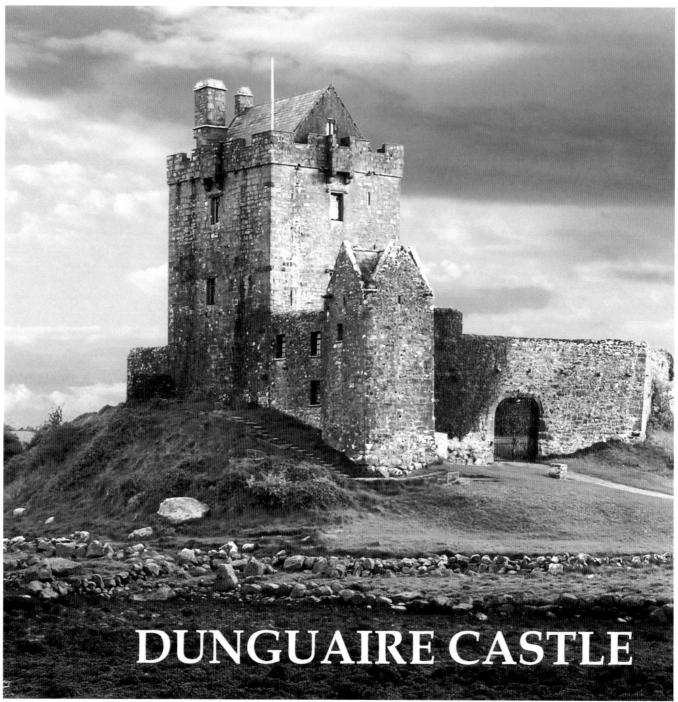

DUNGUAIRE CASTLE

Medieval Banquets on Galway Bay

It is one of the most photographed castles in Ireland, set on a low outcrop of rock along the southern shore of Galway Bay across the small harbor of the little town of Kinvarra. Dunguaire Castle is a single square tower keep confined by a high defensive wall built in 1520 by the celtic Irish Hynes clan. The current castle was built on the spot of an earlier fortress of the 7th Century King Guaire known as "The Generous", son of the legendary King of Connaught, from whom the clan descended. The castle fell into the hands of the Martyns of Galway during the Irish Confederation of the early 1600's and the mayor of Galway lived there until 1642. The rather melancholy setting of the castle, with the mud flats of the bay revealed at low tide, or magnificently hauntingly beautiful when reflected in the bay estuary waters against the ever changing sky when the

tide is in, has been the inspiration of poets and artists. So much so, that the poet and doctor Oliver St John Gogarty purchased the property in 1924 and entertained other poets of his day, including the leaders of the literary Celtic Revival, W.B. Yates, John Millington Synge and George Bernard Shaw. It was Yates who lead the pack, incorporating Celtic traditions into his plays and poems. The castle was later acquired by Lady Ampthill in the 1950's and she was responsible for completing the restoration.

One curious bit of lore about Dunguarie is the generosity of the spirit of the ancient lord of manor. King Guaire acquired his reputation for generosity in pennance for his father's attempted drowning of a mother carrying a child who had been prophesied to take his place. The murder was thwarted when the rock tied to the mother's neck floated rather than sinking. If one stands at the front gate of the castle and asks a question, an answer will be given before the day is over - but beware the Celtic poetic sense of irony and consider well the question before you ask.

The castle is open to visitors from May through September, but it best known for its Medieval Banquets held five nights a week. A four course meal in medieval style, with long wooden bench seating, held in the castle's rather intimate banqueting hall, served by costumed wench waitresses, pouring wine or ale, and entertained by a cast of performers or lords, ladies, knights and jesters, with the culmination of a 40 minute stage show of Irish songs and poems from the famed literati associated with the castle. The medieval banquets at Dunguaire are similar to those at Bunratty Castle closer to Shannon, also operated by Shannon Heritage. Two banquets are held per evening, beginning at 5:30pm and 8:45pm. Reservations are required. You can save a few Euros by booking tickets online. Dunguare Castle is about 30 minutes drive from Shannon or 20 minutes from Galway, easily reached by car along the coastal road of southern Galway Bay on the way toward the famed Moher sea cliffs and the Burren.

O'BRIENS TOWER
CLIFFS OF MOHER

Tourist Castle Tower of Cornelius O'Brien

It is the prime photo spot of the famous cliffs on the west of Ireland. O'Brien's Tower, built in 1835 serves as a frame for poses of strolling cliff oglers and observation point to look down to the giant waves. Not precisely a castle, but perhaps more a "folly", one of the world's first purpose built tourist castle towers. It is named for Cornelius O'Brien, a descendent of the first High King of Ireland, Brian Boru and one of the long line of the O'Brien clan who controlled much of Clare and the west counties. O'Brien owned the lands bordered by the amazing cliffs which drop in sheer magnificence to the roiling sea below and it was he who built the tower which bears his family name and crest, partly as a monument to his heritage, but truly as a tourist attraction.

Today a visitor to the Cliffs of Moher will first encounter the flagstone fences which guard the cliff edge with warning signs not to climb over to the grassy ledge. These fences were not the result of some government safety program, but the result of a wager among landlords. The legendary story goes that O'Brien won a bet with a neighboring landowner that he could construct a wall "six foot high and one inch thick" over a certain distance. The

lesson being, never take a fool's bet. Utilizing the local Liscannor slate flagstones which nearly sprout from the surrounding Burren, he won the wager and the resulting flag fences still stand along the cliff edge. The idea was so impressive, the flat solid flagstones were quickly gathered as building material and used as floor coverings in farmhouses in the 19th century all around Ireland. O'Brien also set up a circular stone table on the sandstone ledge of the cliff to entertain guests who came to see his fence, and more to the point, the cliffs. But with so many curious flocking to the view, the table just wasn't enough.

O'Brien's Tower stands at nearly the highest point of the Cliffs of Moher at 214 meters above the sea at Knockardakin. It was built by O'Brien specifically as an observation deck for the tourism visitors O'Brien believed could boost the local impoverished economy. The tower originally included four separate sections, but due to the ravages of time, salt and sea wind, only the tower and connecting archway remain, restored in 1970. The O'Brien family crest over the arch was added later. When it is open, the tower can be climbed for a viewing point for the cliffs and the Aran Islands. On a clear day, the view from the tower surveys from the coast of Connemara to the north, across Galway Bay and the Clare coastline to Loop Head and the Atlantic beyond, and to the mountains of Kerry to the south. Even when the tower is closed the arch way attracts photographers and visitors for the "Kodak Moment".

O'Brien's passion for building didn't stop with his bet winning fence and tourist's tower. He's responsible for many of the stonework landmarks in County Clare from the mid-19th century, including the bridge over the Inagh River near Liscannor, St Brigid's Well and the St Brigid's National School. A local saying of O'Brien was 'he built everything around here except the cliffs'. Cornelius O'Brien died in 1857 and is buried in the O'Brien Vault in the grave-yard which adjoins St. Brigid's Well.

O'Brien's Tower is free to visit, as are the Cliffs of Moher, sort of. While walking around the cliffs monument does not take an entrance fee, there is a charge for parking in the visitor lot and for entrance to the visitors center. The tower is open to climb at the discretion of the administrators, depending on weather. But a photo in the archway is near unavoidable.

BELFAST CASTLE

Gardens and Views of Belfast Lough

Belfast Castle, set in the hillside slopes of the Cavehill County Park is more 19th Century revival manor house than castle, a genteel replacement for the original castle of Belfast. The first castle was built in the 1600's by Sir Arthur Chichester, the Lord Deputy of Ireland on the site of an earlier Norman fortress which originally stood in the center of what is now Belfast City where the beautiful City Hall now commands High Street. Chichester was a leading figure in the Plantation of Ulster after the "Flight of the Earls" of 1607, and named the Baron of Belfast when it was a relatively modest settlement in the backwater of the bay. Establishing his influence in the north, he was a major force in the founding and expansion of Belfast which began its growth to the capital it is today.

The original castle was destroyed by a devastating fire in 1708. Rather than rebuild the old place in the middle of the growing industrial city, the Chichester descendants picked out a spot in the suburban hills with a commanding view of the city below and waters of the long Belfast Lough to build a new estate. The Belfast Castle which stands today is the 19th Century manor house built by the 3rd Marquess of Donegal, begun on the site about 1860 and

completed in 1870. The mansion was built in the Scottish Baronial style inspired by the royal castle at Balmoral. The castle was designed by Belfast based architect, Charles Lanyon, and given over to the city in 1934 by the the 9th Earl of Shaftesbury.

The castle has a square tower of six floors with corner turrets, with an entrance portico in the Jacobean style. A beautiful external Italianate Renaissance revival spiral staircase to the garden terrace was added in 1894. The castle is used mostly for events, rented out for weddings and private banquets. The Terrace Gardens offer stunning views of the city and bay when the weather is good. The garden is called the "Cat Garden" for the legend that good fortune will come to those who visit the castle as long as there is a cat at the castle. The story goes that there has always been a white cat roaming around the grounds, so the garden has nine different kinds of cats hidden about

to find and count like a feline "Where's Waldo" puzzle, keeping the kids occupied.

A few of the rooms of the upper floors are open to visitors. The Cellar Restaurant in the basement is cozy and styled with the flavor of the Victorian age when the castle was first built. The Castle Tavern bar is open Friday and Saturday nights from 8pm to 10 pm with live music. On the ground floor are an antique and book shop, a small museum and visitor's center.

Made in the USA
Lexington, KY
03 October 2014